Take A City Nature Walk

By Jane Kirkland
with
Rob Kirkland
Dorothy Burke
Melanie Palaisa

You're about to set out on a city nature adventure! You'll be surprised by *what* you find and by *where* you find it. I know because the very first time I took a nature walk in a city I was surprised. I took some city kids on their first nature walk in their own neighborhood city park. Our discoveries were amazing to me.

The tiny park was only one square city block in size. It had some grass, a few trees, an in-ground pool, playground equipment, and a lot of blacktop. I admit I wasn't expecting to find much nature. But as soon as I arrived, I heard a woodpecker. I pointed it out to the kids. They were so excited—none of them had ever seen a woodpecker before!

We found two more species of woodpeckers and lots of other birds that day. We saw insects and worms. We found wildflowers growing through the cracks in the sidewalk. We discovered several different kinds of trees. We watched in awe as a Peregrine Falcon soared above our heads.

The woodpeckers, falcon, insects, worms, trees, and wildflowers had been in the park all along, but the kids never noticed them. All we needed to do was to take the time to stop and look. Nature surprised us that day, and it still surprises me whenever I am in the city. Nature in the city will surprise you, too!

Take Me With You

Every time you take a walk in the city, nature can be very different. The most important thing to remember is to look. The more you look, the more you'll see.

Take this book with you when you visit the city—whether it's a city near your house or a city far away. Take your city nature walk in different seasons to see how many new and different things you can spot.

If you need more paper, take some blank paper or download free city nature forms at our Website, www.takeawalk.com. If you have a pair of binoculars, they'll be helpful for viewing birds.

We saw a male Yellow-bellied Sapsucker just like this one in the city. I like finding this bird anywhere—because I love to say its name!

Nature in the City

There are hundreds of **species** of plants and animals in North American cities. This book teaches you how to find, observe, and identify them. You are currently reading the *Get Ready* section of this book. Here you'll learn a little about cities and about nature in the city.

The *Get Set* section introduces you to three special city residents. Two of them can be found in every city in the world!

Are you surprised to see this raccoon in a city park? The chain on this trash can lid didn't stop it from entering. Wildlife is everywhere and we must find a way to live with it so people and animals are healthy and safe.

The *Go!* section teaches you how to find nature in parks and gardens, on buildings and streets, in parking lots, and near the water. There are pages to take field notes and record your observations and photos to help you identify the species you find. You'll use the Go! section when you are outdoors on your walk.

You can read this book in any order you wish. The important thing to remember is that this book is about your very own experience. It's not about the rainforest or some faraway place you can't visit. It's just not enough to read this book. You need to go outside to explore!

New Word?

Species (SPEE-shees):
A certain kind, variety, or type of living creature.

Please Don't Litter!

Put your trash into trash cans and your recycling into recycling cans. If there are none nearby, carry it with you until you find them.

Staying Safe In the City

Cross Safely

Don't cross the street when the light is red or says "don't walk." This is called jaywalking and it's against the law in many cities.

Please Don't Go Alone

Don't go alone on a nature walk in the city. Take your friends, brothers, sisters, parents, or your entire family with you! It's safer and more fun to discover together.

Please Make Good Choices

Make certain your parents know where you are. Don't go anywhere or do anything your mother wouldn't want you to. Make good choices!

Aniya's Nature

Aniya Hamm, age 8, of Allentown, Pennsylvania, wrote to us and said:

"Nature is a thing that you are not supposed to kill."

We couldn't agree more, Aniya!

What Will You See Today?

If you think there's not much nature to see in the city, think again! You can see three kinds of living things on your nature walk; plants, funguses, and animals. Plants include trees, bushes, grasses, and flowers. Funguses include mushrooms and shelf funguses, which look like shelves growing out of the sides of trees. There are lots of different kinds of animals you might see. You will see vertebrates (VUR-tah-brates) which are animals with backbones, such as birds and mammals. You will see lots of arthropods (AR-throw-pods), such as spiders, insects, scorpions, and crabs. You might see annelids (AN-nel-ids), which are things like earthworms. And you might see mollusks, such as snails, slugs and (if you are near the ocean or some rivers and lakes) clams, oysters, and mussels. Whew! Now do you still think there's not much nature to see in the city?

Where Are the Cockroaches?

You won't find any cockroaches, rats, flies or mosquitoes in this book. Sure, they're part of nature. And they are interesting creatures. My friend, Naturalist Jen Kupp, even keeps cockroaches as pets!

In our cities, cockroaches, rats, houseflies, and mosquitoes are pests. They are always on the lookout for us, because in one way or another we provide lots of food for them. Mostly, we wish these creatures would leave us alone. So we won't go looking for them on our nature walk today. We'll save them for our Take A Walk® book about insects.

Get Ready! Pick a Place...

What is nature? Some say it's everything in the universe that is not man-made. Others say it's every living thing that is "wild." It's a word with a lot of definitions. For the sake of your city nature walk, we'll just say that nature is the wildlife and plants you see in the city today.

Whether you plan to walk in a large city or a small town, you'll find wildlife. But what wildlife? That depends on the location of your city. Let's focus on the wildlife we can find in most cities and towns:

You can find flowers in big city parks, small town gardens, in pots and on windowsills. Wherever you find flowers you're bound to find insects!

birds, insects, mammals, reptiles, and amphibians. Let's pick some plants to look for, too. There are a lot of plants in cities and towns. We'll concentrate on looking for trees and flowers. I suggest trees because they're important and flowers because they're beautiful. If it is wintertime and you're in a cold city, you might not see any flowers, but you can still see the trees.

Expect the unexpected. Red-tailed Hawks like this one (left) can be seen along roadsides all over the U.S. These California Sea Lions (right) are on the wharf in San Francisco.

Big City or Little Town

Every city, big or small, is an *ecosystem* (E-co-sis-tem). An ecosystem is an area where plants, animals, the landscape, and the climate all have an effect on one another. Ecosystems can be large or small. Cities, oceans, forests, and deserts are all ecosystems.

The city is an ecosystem rich with food, water, and space for territories. Much but not all of the food that wild city animals eat is our leftovers. Plants, trees, and man-made structures such as bridges and buildings provide places for wildlife to rest, nest, and seek shelter. Streets and buildings act like heat collectors, making cities warmer than their surrounding areas. The warmer climate allows some species to thrive because they can bloom or lay their eggs earlier. Cities are interesting ecosystems, alive with nature, just waiting for you to discover them.

Wildlife isn't moving into our cities; we're moving into their territory. There's not enough land left for wild things to live in the "wild."

Balance in the Ecosystem

A *native* plant (or animal) is one that grows or lives naturally in a given area or region. It's a species that has not been brought to that region by man. A non-native species is one that has been brought into a region by man. Native plants are good for wildlife. They are the natural food for native wildlife. They also attract the native insects that are the food for native wildlife.

When European settlers first came to North America hundreds of years ago, they brought many of their favorite plants and animals with them, non-native species. But ecosystems require balance—plants and animals must have competitors and predators or their population will grow out of control. Starlings are an example of a non-native bird that has caused a problem for a native bird, the bluebird. Starlings are bigger and more aggressive than bluebirds. They compete with bluebirds for nesting sites in holes in trees and nest boxes. The starlings always win. The bluebird is suffering a major housing shortage.

Today we have many laws that protect our plants and animals so people can't kill them or remove them. But these laws do not apply to non-native species. They protect only our native species.

We now know that it's best to plant only native plants and to bring only native wildlife into a region or the results can be devastating!

Keep in mind that what's native to one area of our country might not be native to all areas.

A Race To Get Home

Pigeons are not native to North America; they were brought here from Europe. Because they aren't native birds, they aren't protected by our wildlife laws. People can (and do) keep pigeons as pets. They often keep them in cages called *coops* on the rooftops of their houses in the city.

Many of these pigeons are used in pigeon races. Those racing pigeons are called homing pigeons. They are bred and trained to be racers. At race time, the pigeons are taken in a cage to a site far away from their homes. When the cage is opened, the pigeons take off and head for home. The pigeon that gets home first wins the race.

So how does the pigeon find its way home? No one is sure, but scientists think that pigeons have a substance called magnetite in their brains that helps them to find the place where they were raised. They're living compasses!

Because of this ability to find their way home, pigeons have been used for over 5,000 years to carry messages. Pigeons were kept away from their home and when a message needed to get to their town, it was put in a tiny pouch and tied to the pigeon's leg. The pigeon was released, and it flew home with the message.

Homing pigeons and wild pigeons look almost alike. A homing pigeon probably has an identification band on its leg. Sometimes a homing pigeon gets lost or hurt and can't get home. If you find one, the number on the band and some research on the Internet will help you find its owner.

Pigeons live in almost every city in the world and they can be a pest to people. They make a mess (and you know what I mean). I'm talking about that white stuff they drop all over the city. There are a lot of pigeons in the city. So, do the math. A lot of pigeons equal a lot of pigeon poop! Maybe that's why there are more pigeons in the city than there are pigeon lovers.

This pigeon is sitting on top of the Empire State Building in New York. What a view!

We call them pigeons but their real name is *Rock Pigeons*. They got this name because they nest on cliffs and high rocks. Do you see any high buildings or bridges made of concrete and steel in your city? Concrete is made from rocks. Maybe they look like cliffs to pigeons. Pigeons eat seeds and grain, and some pigeons live on farms. They eat "human" food like popcorn and bread. They use their beaks like straws when they drink. They feed their young by vomiting a liquid we call "pigeon milk." Yuck! Pigeons mate for life.

Pigeons have seven different forms, or *morphs*. One morph (not shown) is the "spread" morph which is mostly black The others are shown below and on the bottom of page 7. From left to right below are the "blue-bar," the "checker" (which has a checkered pattern on its wings) and the "pied" morphs.

Pigeons Everywhere?

Personally, I like pigeons, although I wish there weren't so many to like! I like the way their heads bob back and forth when they walk. Their "cooing" reminds me of a cat purring. It's a very pretty sound. I think pigeons are fun to watch, too.

One day when I was in the city waiting for a traffic light to change, a pigeon stood next to me on the sidewalk. It didn't cross the road until the light changed! I laughed so hard I missed my green light.

Why did the pigeon wait for the light to change before crossing the road? Because only jays can jaywalk, silly!

Aren't pigeons interesting? I think my favorite thing about the pigeon is that the male's neck is more iridescent (ear-a-DES-cent) than the female's neck. The male's neck can look shiny purple and even pink! And those feet! A pigeon's legs and feet can be gray-black, red, or pink! If everyone knew what you now know about pigeons, maybe more people would love them.

These three pigeon morphs are the "red," the "red-bar," and the "white." People call white pigeons "doves." Doves represent peace in many cultures of the world. .

Meet Jack's Pigeons

Pigeons, pigeons, pigeons. The pigeons I've met are very entertaining—they make funny little noises, flap their wings, and squabble over food. They come in lots of colors—green, blue, silver, gray, etc. One thing that I don't like is that they have red eyes. Other than that, they're funny!

*Jack Wooldridge, age 9,
Great Meadows, New Jersey*

Youngster or Adult?

When young pigeons leave their nests they look like adults. But you can tell young pigeons by the color of their eyes and their cere (**SEER**). The cere is the fleshy piece on the upper part of the beak. It's gray in young birds, white in adults. Their eyes are brown or gray for about eight months, then they turn to red or orange-red.

Red eyes, white cere. Adult or youngster?

A pigeon hitched a ride on my husband Rob's backpack in Paris, France. Which morph is it?

New Word?

Pesticide (PES-ti-side):

A chemical used to destroy pesky weeds or insects.

How'd We Get These Pictures?

I felt like the luckiest person in the world when I received permission to photograph this Peregrine Falcon banding—until I learned that the nest was inside a girder on the underside of a huge bridge. I no longer felt so lucky. I don't like heights. I admit it. But I really wanted photos for this book. So I asked my friend Kevin Loughlin, a wildlife photographer, to help. He agreed to take the pictures. While Kevin and the banders were high on the bridge, I took pictures from the ground with my sister Midge and my feet firmly planted! Kevin took this photo (below) from the bridge of us standing by my car. See how far up they were?

I'm very grateful to Kevin for taking these fabulous pictures for you and to Dan Brauning of the Pennsylvania Game Commission for giving us this once-in-a-lifetime opportunity.

Can you see me way down there on the ground?

Peregrine Falcons are one of the most exciting birds that live in our cities. But they weren't originally a city bird. So why did they move in? Scientists brought them to our cities to save the species.

Falcons build their nest on ledges like cliffs, bridges and buildings. This one is inside the girder of a bridge.

Peregrines were once *endangered,* meaning that their population numbers were so low that, if we did nothing, the species may have gone extinct. Peregrines faced many problems; the biggest was a ***pesticide*** called DDT. When DDT gets into a Peregrine's system, it weakens the shells of their eggs. The eggs are crushed by the parents when they sit on them. The chicks can't survive. If scientists hadn't stepped in, the falcon might be extinct today.

Matt Sharp, of the Academy of Natural Sciences in Philadelphia, prepares to band a young chick.

Art McMorris checks the bird and records information about its size and health before returning it to the nest.

Peregrine Falcons

DDT was banned in the 1970s in the U.S. At the same time, scientists began breeding Peregrine Falcons so they could release the young birds into the "wild." They chose cities as the release sites. Cities have plenty of food (such as pigeons), shelter, and places for roosting and nesting.

Today, the Peregrine population is on the rise. But they are not out of danger. DDT is still used in parts of South America where our falcons migrate. Traces of it can still be found in the tissues and eggs of Peregrine Falcons. You can learn more about falcons and about how you can help by searching for "Peregrine Falcon" on the Web.

Art McMorris removed the chicks from the nest and wore a helmet to protect him from the adult birds. Matt Sharp weighed the chicks one at a time by placing them in a white bag hanging from a scale.

Both of the Peregrine parents attended the nest and fed the chicks. They were very upset when the chicks were removed for banding. They even swooped down at the banders. Falcons can reach speeds of more than 200 miles per hour when they dive.

Why Do We Band Peregrines?

I asked Dr. Art McMorris to explain why we band falcons. Here's what he said:

Where do young Peregrine Falcons go once they've left the nest? How long do they live? Where were their parents born? How do we find out? We (Dr. Art McMorris of the Pennsylvania Game Commission and his supervisor Daniel Brauning) are studying these questions. We monitor breeding pairs of Peregrine Falcons and band the young at the nest. Each bird receives a light aluminum "bracelet" with a unique number. If the bird is found again, we'll know exactly which bird it is, where it came from, and how old it is. But most banded birds are not found again until they die. How can we know where it traveled and lived during its lifetime? Many birds are also given a color band on the other leg. These bands have a number and letter which can be read with good binoculars or a telescope, so birds can be identified and tracked while living free. Sometimes a small transmitter is placed on the bird to track the bird by satellite from anywhere on earth. In 2002 the Pennsylvania Game Commission fitted four young Peregrine Falcons with solar-powered satellite transmitters, allowing them to be tracked as they traveled and explored their world.

The more we know about the birds and their activities, the more we can help them survive and return to a stable population. Learn more at:

pgc.state.pa.us
peregrinefund.org

Washington, DC, holds a Cherry Blossom Festival every spring when more than 3700 cherry trees bloom in the city.

Arbor Day Foundation

The National Arbor Day Foundation is the largest tree-planting environmental organization in the world. They educate people about trees, and they sponsor a program called "Tree City USA." To be named a "Tree City USA" a city or town must meet certain requirements. Those requirements include a budget to take care of trees and an Arbor Day observance to celebrate trees. Do you live in a Tree City USA?

Every year the National Arbor Day Foundation also sponsors a poster contest for 5th graders all over the U.S. The theme of their contest is "Trees are Terrific." In 2004 David Zander of Snohomish, Washington, won the contest with his poster about terrific trees in cities and towns. Congratulations, David!

To learn more about The National Arbor Day Foundation, visit:

arborday.org

What if you could give an award for a city's most important plant? Which plant would you choose? I would choose trees! I think trees are the most important plants that grow in the city.

Trees provide food, shelter, and building material. They take in carbon dioxide and give us oxygen. They help to keep the soil from eroding, block traffic noise, and create shade.

In the winter, evergreens provide shelter and protection for animals and they keep our houses warmer by blocking the wind. During summer in the city, the buildings, roads, and traffic all create heat. The city can become very hot. Trees help to cool it down by making shade and holding moisture. Trees can reduce the cost to cool our houses, saving us money.

Trees line the streets of many of our cities, like this one in New York City. They help to block traffic noise and create shade. Can you see the shade from the trees?

Dogwood trees are popular in cities and towns. Many towns celebrate with Dogwood Festivals when the dogwoods bloom in the spring.

Most Important Plant

When you see a tree, how will you tell which species it is? Examine it and see if you can find it in this book or in a field guide. Look at the overall shape of the tree. Does it have a round top, or is it tall and skinny? Look at the color of the leaves. Look at the leaves—are they flat or needle shaped? The color and texture of the bark are important things to notice. Is the bark scaley or smooth? Use your ID pages to write down your observations.

Trees provide food and nesting sites to many animals, like this squirrel (above). They bring smiles to people's faces and sometimes (below) they even smile back!

I'm not the only one who thinks trees are important. We celebrate trees in many ways—on Arbor Day, Earth Day, and at Dogwood and Cherry Blossom Festivals. We even have a state tree for every state in the U.S. What's yours?

Trees in the Zoo?

When you visit the zoo to see the animals, don't forget to look at the trees. Like the animals, trees are very well cared for at the zoo. Many zoos label their plants and trees, so that you won't need a field guide to identify them. Yes, even the zoo is a great place for a nature walk. The plants and trees attract many of the free-roaming local city residents (and I don't mean the people).

Roman's Trees

Big as a house
Brown body
Green on top that looks like clouds
Grown from a seed
Thick trunk
An animal's home

Roman Rodriguez, age 9,
Milwaukee, Wisconsin

Gone Surfing!

You can learn more information about nature from these organizations:

The National Audubon Society

audubon.org

The National Wildlife Federation

enature.com

nwf.org

National Geographic Kids

nationalgeographic.com/kids

I Agree with Mr. Wright

Frank Lloyd Wright, one of the most famous architects of our time, once said:

"Study nature, love nature, stay close to nature. It will never fail you."

Field Guides for You

A field guide will help you to identify the wildlife and plants you find in the city. Listed here are four field guides I recommend. Look through them at your local bookstore and choose the one you like best. Personally, I like them all, but you only need one!

Roadside Wildflowers
A Peterson Flash Guide™ written by Roger Tory Peterson, published by Houghton Mifflin. More than 100 species of the most common wildflowers found along the roadsides of the U.S. and Canada.

Urban Wildlife
A Pocket Naturalist™ Guide written by James Kavanagh, published by Waterford Press. Color Illustrations, covers North America.

Urban Wildlife
A Peterson First Guide® written by Roger Tory Peterson, published by Houghton Mifflin. Color illustrations, covers North America.

DK Pockets: Trees
Written by Theresa Greenaway published by DK Pub Merchandise. An easy-to-use and easy-to-carry field guide to trees of North America.

Today you are an Urban (ER-ban) Ecologist (ee-KALL-uh-jist). *Urban* means *city*. An ecologist is a person who studies the relationships between living things and their environment. So an Urban Ecologist is a person who studies the relationship between living things and their environment in the city. That's what you're doing today, isn't it?

You might want to take *field notes*. Scientists, artists and others who study nature (like me) take field notes. Field notes help us to remember our

Look for European Starlings today like this one shown in its summer breeding colors. In the winter they have black bills and are heavily speckled in white, making them look paler.

outdoor observations. We use field notes to record a detailed description of the things we saw and where we saw them. We include other information, too, such as the date, a description of the weather, and our location.

If you take notes each time you explore you can compare your notes from different seasons. By comparing your notes, you can see how nature changes with the seasons. You can even compare your notes when you take walks in the same season.

Today you're an Urban Ecologist. The city is your *field*.

Field Notes

Your Field Notes Page:

You can use this form or you can use blank paper for your Field Notes. If you need more forms you can download them for free at our website. Your field notes should include today's date and your location (the name of the city, the street, or the park you are exploring). Fill in the time of day you are walking. Write about today's weather: the temperature, what the sky looks like, and so forth. You can also use this form to list the plants and wildlife you see. Write what you can now, and then add more during and after your walk.

Need more room to draw or write? Use blank paper or download free forms at www.takeawalk.com.

What's Your Favorite Park?

Cities have many different kinds of parks, such as ball parks, industrial parks, recreational parks, memorial parks (cemeteries), dog parks and historical parks. There are parks where people go to relax, like a city park with trees and benches and ponds and fountains. There are nature parks and wilderness parks, which are especially for enjoying nature. You can guess which are my favorite kinds of parks, can't you? Which are your favorites?

Bruce's Trees

This book is dedicated to Bruce Glenn, age 11, of Philadelphia, Pennsylvania. He was an inspiration to me during one of my very first nature walks in the city. You can read the dedication on the inside front cover. Here's a note from Bruce:

"I like taking little adventures in the park. Whether I'm squirrel watching or just feeding birds. But I really like looking at trees and finding old tree leaves and comparing them to others that have fallen days before."

Dragonflies in Central Park

When I was taking photographs for this book I visited Central Park, New York. I was surprised to find hundreds of Common Darner Dragonflies in huge groups. It was their migration season. What a fantastic sight!

City parks are good places for a nature walk. A city park bench is like the seat in a movie theater. Sit on one, look around, and before you know it you'll be enjoying a real-life nature movie—and the stars of that movie will probably be birds. Birds in the city are used to being close to humans. You can observe them closely from a park bench. But don't get too comfortable. There's more to explore!

Sit on a park bench like my friends Henry and Alex, and you become the audience to nature's show.

Walk around the park. Remember to move slowly if you are watching an animal. You don't want to scare it away before you've had a chance to get a good look. Don't let an animal see you staring at it or it might think it's going to be your dinner and leave! Be patient. Keep a safe distance. Move slowly.

There are 17 species of chipmunks in the western U.S. but only one in the east. This one has enough food in its cheeks to feed them all!

I've visited city parks all around the world. I'm convinced that statues are real people who like to wear living bird hats!

In a City Park

Stay away from large crowds so you can listen for animals and insects. Your ears can help you to find nature, too! Look on the ground for chipmunks, mice, rabbits and other mammals. Look for insects on the ground, too. If you see ants, observe them for a few minutes and you'll see how they are always so busy! Study any groups of birds you see on the ground or in the air to determine if there is more than one species in the group. Look in trees for nests. See if you can find and tell the difference between a bird's nest and a squirrel's nest. A squirrel's nest looks like a big ball of leaves. Look for holes in tree trunks. Some birds make nests in those holes so look for birds flying in and out.

Remember that different seasons offer different sightings. In the spring look for new plant growth. In the summer focus on insects. In the fall look for leaves changing color. In the winter, look for any signs of food, like berries or nuts, and there you'll find animals.

Parks are a good place to see hawks like this Red-tailed Hawk flying overhead in search of food.

The fun of a nature walk is the observation. Don't make this a race to see how many things you can see. Instead, take the time to observe carefully each thing you see so you can learn about its behavior and so you can recognize it more easily the next time you see it. Take notes to help you remember what you saw and what it looked like.

Let It Be

A city is an ecosystem. Leave plants and animals where you find them. If you remove them, they will probably die. Everything you put into and move out of an ecosystem has an affect on the entire ecosystem.

Pale Male in Central Park

If you like reading about nature in the city, you'll love **Red-Tails in Love: a Wildlife Drama in Central Park.**

This book is a true story about Pale Male, a Red-tailed Hawk that lives and hunts in New York City's Central Park. For several years people have come from all over the United States to get a glance of Pale Male or to watch him raise his chicks in a nest high upon a Fifth Avenue apartment building. You'll enjoy learning about Pale Male, the birds of Central Park, and the bird-watchers, too!

Red-Tails in Love: A Wildlife Drama in Central Park.

Written by Marie Winn. Published by Vintage Publishing.

Go! Look for Nature...

What Goes In Must Come Out

Don't throw anything into the drainage ditches and grates you see along the streets (like the one in the crow cartoon below). Whatever gets thrown into them gets sent directly to the local natural water supplies. This is just one of the ways our lakes, rivers and reservoirs get polluted.

Treyvonn's Peregrine

*Dark spooky woods
trees fallen down.
Sudden tail swoops
dark mustache facing me.
I am delighted seeing
a Peregrine Falcon
with its staring eye.
I'll carry this with me for life.*

Treyvonn Brown-Nance
Age 9
Milwaukee, Wisconsin

You can find crows in the city. One day I watched a crow as it shook open a crumpled up fast food bag on the side-walk. When it got the bag open it pulled out a half-full container of French fries. That was one smart crow!

Even if you don't go looking for nature, it can find you, and sometimes in the most unusual places. It found me in the cell phone store at the mall in town. I was talking with a saleswoman when suddenly an insect flew past my face. "Oh, sorry," the saleswoman said. "We've been trying to kill that bug all day." The insect landed on a light on the ceiling. I could see it was a dragonfly. I was so upset watching it hit the ceiling as it tried to escape. But there was no

We found a birds nest on this sign in a city multi-level parking garage.

way out! I had to help it. I asked the saleswoman for a broom. I held the end of the broom near the ceiling next to the dragonfly. I stood very still for a few minutes until the dragonfly crawled onto the end of the broom.

Then I very carefully lowered the broom and walked slowly toward the front door. My husband Rob walked ahead of me to clear the way as we walked through the mall to the exit. All the while

This Canada Goose made a nest in a vacant lot right next to the road.

the tired dragonfly stayed on the broom. Once outside, I placed the broom on the dirt at the base of a tree (away from the walkway) and the dragonfly fell off. Later I went back to check on it and the dragonfly was gone. Dragonflies in the mall—who knew?

On Man-Made Structures

What nature can you find in parking lots? Birds, like gulls, sparrows, starlings and crows, just to name a few. The surface of parking lots gets warm and the street lights provide high places for birds to perch.

Look on buildings for signs and lights where birds might be nesting or just resting. Look on the sides of buildings for moths or other insects, as well as lizards, wasp nests and bird nests.

Look on sidewalks for worms after a heavy rain. Look for plants and flowers forcing their way up to the sunlight through the cracks in the pavement. Insects crawl in and out of the cracks, too. Trees drop seeds and fruits on sidewalks and streets, attracting many kinds of animals and insects.

Like this gull, some birds perch high on light posts to get a good look at the world.

Check out the roadsides and abandoned lots for wildflowers, butterflies, and other insects. You can see hawks in trees. Alongside roads you can see mammals like rabbits, deer, and groundhogs grazing in grassy areas.

These two Silver-spotted Skippers are on a plant called Bull Thistle, along-side roads. The skippers are butter-flies, not moths, and the plant is a prickly wildflower.

Naturescaping Broward County

A NatureScape is a beautiful landscape that is also an urban wildlife habitat. It contains food, water, shelter, and places for wildlife to raise their young. NatureScaping uses native plants. Native plants require less water and less care in general than non-native plants. This creates a healthier environment for insects, birds, wildlife, and people, too.

Broward County, Florida, is asking residents and businesses to protect the environment in South Florida—including the Everglades—by NatureScaping their properties.

The National Wildlife Federation has a program to certify NatureScapes. Thousands of homes in the U.S. have gotten their NatureScapes certified. But never has an entire county been certified. Broward County wants to be the first. To reach that goal, the County must have 1300 certified homes and businesses. About 800 are certified already! We wish Broward County good luck. Learn more about NatureScapes at the National Wildlife Federation's website:

nwf.org

Langston's Peregrine

I walk through the city, a shadow follows.
I run and run. The shadow is gone.
I come to an open area. I see something. A bird!
Not any bird—A Peregrine Falcon. Gray flashing feathers. I just stand. Then it flaps its mystic wings. It flies away.

Langston Peoples, age 9
Milwaukee, Wisconsin

Forget Ladybugs!

My friend John Laskowski knows more about moths than any person I know. He's a moth expert and he visits schools to teach people about moths. John loves insects and he gets upset whenever people call the Ladybird Beetle a "Ladybug" because that's not its real name! John thinks our poets are to blame for this nickname. So John wrote this poem for our book:

> Though a famous poet said it,
> Called the Ladybird beetle
> A Ladybug—I dread it!
> So please state it correctly.
> He couldn't find the words
> To rhyme with beetle
> So he changed it to bug.
> Now to him I must needle
> And call him a slug!

John D. Laskowski, The Mothman

mothman.org

Butterfly Gardens

Butterfly gardens feature two types of native plants. One type is the host plant which is the plant the caterpillars eat before they become butterflies. The other type is the nectar plant which provides food for the adult butterflies. Butterfly houses are indoor butterfly gardens—inside a structure with walls and doors. There you can see many species of butterflies up close. Sometimes they'll even land on you. Butterfly houses usually include species that are not native to where you live, so you'll see species you wouldn't otherwise see. Is there a butterfly garden or butterfly house in your city?

Most cities have several kinds of gardens. There are small gardens and large gardens. There are free gardens and gardens you must pay an admission fee to see. There are gardens in people's yards and gardens-in-a-box, beautiful flowers in window boxes.

Large gardens have more than just beautiful flowers. They have plants and trees. Sometimes they have fountains,

The spring is a great time to find flowers in the city. Some grow naturally. Others, like these, are planted.

statues and ponds. You can find lots of wildlife: insects, birds, spiders, and mammals. The wildlife is attracted to a garden because it is a source of food and protection. Insects come for the plants and flowers. Spiders come for the insects. Birds come for spiders, insects, seeds and nectar. Mammals come for the plants or insects. From a distance gardens look peaceful and quiet. They look as if they are paintings. Everything seems to be standing still. But explore up close and you might find a garden as busy and crowded as a city!

What's the name of this insect? It visits gardens and eats other insects called aphids. It may look like a ladybug but you'd better read "Forget Ladybugs" in the sidebar.

Treasures of City Gardens

Gardens give us the opportunity to get very close to nature and to see the many relationships in nature. One such interesting relationship is the one between bees and flowers. Bees and flowers help each other. Bees collect nectar and pollen from flowers—it's their food. As bees move from flower to flower, some of the pollen they collected at one flower drops off onto another flower, pollinating it.

You can see the pollen on the head of this bee. Some will fall off as it travels from flower to flower.

When you explore a garden, be sure to look in shady spots and sunny spots. (Please stay on the paths.) Some plants and animals need sun, some need shade. Plants such as ferns grow in the shade and insects such as butterflies need the sun to warm them up so they can fly. If you discover a butterfly rest-ing in the sun, don't block the sunlight. If you do, it might move away to a sunnier spot. Let the sun continue to shine on it as you approach quietly and slowly, and you'll be able to observe it closely.

Flowers attract many insects, like these Japanese Beetles (top photo) and Monarch butterfly (bottom photo). The beetles are natives of Japan. The Monarch is drinking nectar from a plant called a Butterfly Bush.

Urban Ecology Careers

There are too many careers that focus on urban ecology to list in this space. But here are a few you might want to consider. Keep one thing in mind; science is very important in this field so keep your science grades up. Of course, you'll also need to keep your math grades up and, heck, just keep working hard in all areas of school and you'll be able to choose whatever career you want to have! Even athletes have to read their contracts so keep up your reading skills, too!

Landscape Architects (LAND-skape AR-ki-tekts) design areas like parks, shopping centers, golf courses, and college campuses. They plan where buildings, roads and walkways go and how to arrange flowers, shrubs and trees so they are both functional and pleasing to the eye.

Wildlife Ecology and Conservation Professionals work to understand and manage wildlife and their habitats to help them survive.

Urban Forest Landscapers manage the existing trees in a city. They study how trees can help people who live and work in the city and how people can help the trees.

Community and Regional Planning Professionals create programs to improve the quality of life in our communities. They focus on how we use our land in those communities.

Go! Discover Nature...

What's a Watershed?

The water from your faucet might come from a well, or it might be supplied by your water company. It is hopefully clean, safe water. But where does the water come from originally? It comes from your watershed!

Water doesn't stand still. Water flows underground and from small streams into bigger creeks, rivers, or lakes. A watershed is the area that the water travels over and through on its way to a larger body of water. A watershed includes the land, and the water that runs through it, as well as the plants, animals, and humans who live there. Did you know that you live in a watershed? The health of the water you drink, bathe in, and do your laundry in depends on the health of your watershed. To find which watershed you live in, ask your teacher or parents or go to:

epa.gov/surf

Like a Duck Out of Water.

Sometimes you see ducks and geese out of water walking with their young lined up behind them. This happens a lot when they cross the road. Why? To get the other side, silly!

There are many different bodies of water in and around our cities: lakes, ponds, rivers, streams, canals and creeks. Some cities are even located near the ocean. Explore different bodies of water to see different plants and animals.

Look for insects hopping, flying, or swimming in or on the water. Dragonflies lay their eggs on the water. When they hatch, they live in the water as nymphs—some as long as several years, shedding their skins many times as they grow. When they are adults, they fly near the water looking for mates. Dragonflies are food for birds, fish, frogs, spiders, and many other species.

Look at puddles after a rain. You might see small birds or butterflies bathing or drinking.

Sometimes it's hard to tell the difference between Green Frogs (above) and Bullfrogs. But only Green Frogs have ridges on their backs. Painted Turtles (below) can often be seen in groups basking on logs or stones.

In and Around the Water

Ponds are often good places to see frogs and turtles. Frogs are very sensitive to their environment—they cannot survive around polluted water or polluted land. Don't pick up or move turtles, frogs, or anything else. Many species are dropping in numbers because of loss of habitat. Everything needs to stay in its habitat to survive.

When the seasons change, so do the plants and animals you see. What you see on your walk today is different than what you'll see when you return on a different day, month, or season. An ecosystem is always changing.

Many types of birds can be found near water. Look for *wading birds, waterfowl,* and *marsh birds.* Wading Birds, like this Great Blue Heron (left), have long legs and wade (walk) in shallow water looking for food like snakes, frogs, and fish. Waterfowl, such as Canada Geese (above) and Mallards, live in or near the water. Both Mallards and Canada Geese eat by sticking their heads under water and their butts up in the air. I like to call this "duck butting". I don't recommend this unless you're a duck! Marsh birds, like this Yellow-headed Blackbird (top right—a western bird) and this Red-winged Blackbird (bottom right—an eastern bird), live in and around wetlands.

Lashawn's Riddle

I sleep in the morning, I come out at night. My eyes light up like a flashlight. I also sleep upside down and sleep in a cave or a tree. I come in all sizes. What am I?

Lashawn Gillispie, age 10, Milwaukee, Wisconsin (Answer: A bat!)

It's a Lot to Clean Up!

The New York Restoration Project buys vacant lots and turns them into neighborhood gardens. They are a good example of what one city and many volunteers can do to make a difference. To learn more:

nyrp.org

Alexandra's Imagination

Today I went to Boat House Row to go on a nature walk. I thought I saw a whale in the river. My imagination went wild. It really, really looked like a whale. I saw a wide black bump. It was sleek and shiny because of the sunshine. There was a white patch around its eyes and it looked like it was swimming up and down because of the waves. On top of the whale was a tall, white bird. It was just standing there looking around. Remember to use your imagination on every nature walk. It makes it more fun!

Alexandra Lacouture, age 8, Harleysville, Pennsylvania

Crow Calls

We have two kinds of crows in North America; the American Crow and the Fish Crow. How can you tell the difference? By their call. The American crow has a call that sounds like "Caw Caw." The Fish Crow call sounds like "AW-oh."

Jalen's Crows

*Dark black
Sharp, pointed beak.
Beady eyes.
Wings as black as its belly.
Intelligent enough to fly away from predators.
Caw Caw Caw!
Call of the Crow.*

*Jalen Perry
Age 9,
Milkwaukee,
Wisconsin.*

Here's an example of how to use your Nature ID Page. Taking good notes about your observations while you are in the field will help you to remember what you saw. If it's a species you don't recognize, your notes will help you to identify the species when you research it in your field guide, at the library, or on the Web.

Circle one (if you know it)

This is a Plant Bird Mammal Amphibian Reptile Insect Spider

Habitat and location. I saw it in a tree in the park on 23rd and Market Streets.

Size and physical description. It was about 8" tall and it was gray with a bushy tail. It had a white belly.

Behavior Observation (if it is an animal). It was very noisy and it was gathering nuts.

Additional Notes. It twitched its tail a lot.

Species Name. Eastern Gray Squirrel

Sara Kuch, 14, of Coatesville, Pennsylvania, drew this Eastern Gray Squirrel. It looks just like one I saw in my park. Thanks, Sara!

22

Nature ID Page.

Circle one (if you know it)

This is a Plant Bird Mammal Amphibian Reptile Insect Spider

Habitat and location.

Size and physical description.

Behavior Observation (if it is an animal).

Additional Notes.

Species Name.

(Optional) Make a drawing here:

Key Word Search

If you like to use your computer to do research and learn more about nature in the city, try searching for these words and phrases:

Urban Ecology

Nature in the City

Urban Wildlife

Environment

Urban Parks

Need more room to draw or write? Use blank paper or download free forms at www.takeawalk.com.

23

Go! Identify Urban Birds

Here are some common North American urban birds not pictured elsewhere in this book. Some of these birds cannot be seen in all parts of the U.S.

Ring-billed Gull

Mute Swan

Mallard (male)

Mallard (female)

Mourning Dove

Downy Woodpecker

Blue Jay

American Crow

Black-capped Chickadee

Northern Mockingbird

House Finch

House Sparrow (Male)

House Sparrow (Female)

American Robin

Common Grackle

This is a selection of leaves from some of the most common trees found in North American cities. Not all of these trees are found in all parts of the U.S.

White Oak

Red Oak

American Sycamore
(Fall colors)

White Mulberry

Red Maple
(Fall colors)

Redbud

Quaking Aspen
(Fall colors)

Ginkgo

White Poplar

Cottonwood

Ailanthus

Honey Locust

Artists from left to right:

Natalie Mercado, age 8,
Allentown, Pennsylvania.

Nick Mecca, age 8,
Drexel Hill, Pennsylvania.

Nefalga Lewis, age 8,
New York City.

Go! Identify Urban Insects and Spiders

This is a selection of some of the most common urban insects and spiders found in North America. In addition to these you can find insects on pages 17, 18 and 19.

Red-legged Grasshopper

Cricket

Firefly

Common Green Darner

Black-winged Damselfly

Bald-faced Hornet

Honey Bee

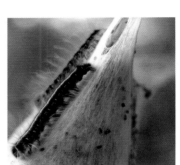
Eastern Tent Caterpillar

Mourning Cloak

Cabbage White Butterfly

Brown Daddy Longlegs

Garden Spider

Artists from left to right:

Shruti Nadkarni, age 10, Edison, New Jersey.

Shree Nadkarni, age 6, Edison, New Jersey.

Tiana Crawford, age 10, New York City.

Go! Identify Urban Flowers

This is a selection of some of the most common flowers found in North America. You can find some of these flowers in gardens throughout the city. Others are wildflowers. Not all of these flowers grow in all areas of the U.S.

Black-eyed Susans

Chicory

Pansies

Daisy Fleabane

Coneflower

Red Clover

Crown Vetch

Impatiens

Roses

Queen Anne's Lace

Marigolds

Tulips

Daylily

Dandelion

Dandelion

Go! Identify Urban Reptiles and Amphibians

This is a selection of some of the most common reptiles and amphibians that can be found in North American cities. Not all of these are found in all areas of the U.S.

Box Turtle

Snapping Turtle

Red-eared Slider

Spotted Salamander

Northern Leopard Frog

Green Treefrog

Bullfrog

American Toad

Northern Water Snake

Garter Snake

Eastern Fence Lizard

Green Anole

City Park

Leaf piles in the streets,
Children picking up lady bugs,
Chickadees getting in your business.
Collecting fossils that have been in the lake for years.
Horns distracting you
From the sky of green and blue colors.

Josephina Sances, age 10,
Milwaukee, Wisconsin

Squirrels

Climbing up the tree, like a brown creeper,
Or down, like a nuthatch.
Crawling, they suddenly appear.
They're always watching.
A secret spy, squirming, hopping
From branch to branch.

Isabella Sances, age 10,
Milwaukee, Wisconsin

This is a selection of some of the most common urban mammals found in North America. Others are pictured throughout this book. Not all of these mammals are found in all areas of the U.S.

White-footed Mouse

Eastern Cottontail

Black-tailed Jackrabbit

Eastern Gray Squirrel

Armadillo

Beaver

Groundhog (Woodchuck)

Striped Skunk

Eastern Red Fox

Coyote

Virginia Opossum

White-tailed Deer

The cityscape on the left was drawn by Haley Fitzgerald, age 10, of King of Prussia, Pennsylvania. The city park scene on the right was drawn by Cidney James, age 10, of New York City.

From Milwaukee Wisconsin

What do you do with an abandoned, polluted park filled with crime and trash? It depends on who you are. In 1990, city officials in Milwaukee suggested the idea of building condominiums to solve the problem, but the local residents had a very different idea. They took it into their own hands to clean up tons of garbage and scrape graffiti off trees. They dug up invasive plants and planted beautiful prairies. The residents believed that criminals and lawbreakers would not want to be in a busy park filled with people. Too many witnesses! Their idea worked. Soon volunteer naturalists began leading central city school children on walks in the park. Dog walkers and bikers began to visit the area as well. Today, the park has evolved into the Urban Ecology Center (www.urbanecologycenter.org). The center is an environmental educational place for both children and adults. More than 15,000 students and 10,000 adults visit the center every year. The land has become an outdoor classroom for grade schools, a field research station for universities, and a natural sanctuary for the local residents. The revitalization project has been good for all life in this urban neighborhood—wildlife and humans alike.

*Ken Leinbach
Executive Director of the Urban
Ecology Center of Milwaukee*

urbanecologycenter.org

People all over the world have realized that time is running out if we are going to preserve our plants and wildlife for our own future. And people are starting to do something about it! Read the stories of two special city projects in the sidebars of these pages. Milwaukee, Wisconsin, turned a terrible place into a beautiful wildlife refuge. Chattanooga, Tennessee, used to be one of the dirtiest cities in the United States—but not today! I bet it pleases you to learn that people are making a difference.

Can you believe this beautiful scene (above) is in the City of Milwaukee? Chattanooga (below) used to be one of the dirtiest cities in our nation. Remember, cities are ecosystems that need our help to be healthy. Chattanooga and Milwaukee are just two of the many cities that are making a difference. Is yours?